The MASS BOOK

A Redemptorist Publication

The MASS BOOK

Published by:
Redemptorist Publications
A Registered Charity limited by guarantee. Registered in England 3261721

Editor: Francis Dickinson, C.SS.R.
Illustrations: The Benedictine Nuns of Cockfosters

Thirty-fifth printing July 2000 (409th thousand)

Acknowledgements:
New English translation of the Order of Mass and Eucharistic Prayers copyright © 1969, International Committee on English in the Liturgy Inc. All rights reserved.

Concordat cum originali:
Fr John Dewis
31st January 1975

Approval for Scotland: The Mass Book agrees with the original and is approved for use in Scotland.
John Symon,
Secretary of the National Liturgy Commission for Scotland.

ISBN 0 85231 165 6

Production: Paul Kennedy Print & Publishing Keighley

Redemptorist
PUBLICATIONS
Alphonsus House Chawton Hampshire GU34 3HQ
Telephone 01420 88222 Fax 01420 88805
rp@redempt.org www.redempt.org

The Order of Mass

Introductory Rites

A HYMN or a Psalm may be sung while the Priest comes to the altar, or the ENTRY ANTIPHON said or sung.

GREETING THE PEOPLE

All make the sign of the cross as the Priest says:

Priest: In the name of the Father, and of the Son, and of the Holy Spirit.

Congregation: **Amen.**

The Priest greets the people in one of these ways:

P: The grace of our Lord Jesus Christ and the love of God and the fellowship of the Holy Spirit be with you all.

or

The grace and peace of God our Father and the Lord Jesus Christ be with you.

or

The Lord be with you.

C: **And also with you.**

The Priest may now say a few words about the Mass theme of the day.

THE PENITENTIAL RITE

One of the following Acts of Penance is now said.

---

1 *P:* My brothers and sisters, (or some similar greeting) to prepare ourselves to celebrate the sacred mysteries, let us call to mind our sins.

(Pause)

P & C: **I confess to almighty God,**
and to you, my brothers and sisters,
that I have sinned through my own fault
(All strike their breast)
in my thoughts and in my words,
in what I have done,
and in what I have failed to do;
and I ask blessed Mary, ever virgin,
all the angels and saints,
and you, my brothers and sisters,
to pray for me to the Lord our God.

P: May almighty God have mercy on us,
forgive us our sins,
and bring us to everlasting life.
C: **Amen.**

P: Lord, have mercy.
C: **Lord, have mercy.**

P: Christ, have mercy.
C: **Christ, have mercy.**

P: Lord, have mercy.
C: **Lord, have mercy.**

(Turn to page 6)

---

2 *P:* My brothers and sisters, (or some similar greeting) to prepare ourselves to celebrate the sacred mysteries, let us call to mind our sins.

(Pause)

P: Lord, we have sinned against you:
Lord, have mercy.
C: **Lord, have mercy.**

P: Lord, show us your mercy and love.
C: **And grant us your salvation.**

P: May almighty God have mercy on us,
forgive us our sins,
and bring us to everlasting life.
C: **Amen.**

P: Lord, have mercy.
C: **Lord, have mercy.**

P: Christ, have mercy.
C: **Christ, have mercy.**

P: Lord, have mercy.
C: **Lord, have mercy.**

(Turn to page 6)

---

3 *P:* My brothers and sisters, (or some similar greeting)
to prepare ourselves to celebrate the sacred
mysteries, let us call to mind our sins.

(Pause, followed by these or similar invocations)

P: You were sent to heal the contrite:
Lord, have mercy.
C: **Lord, have mercy.**

P: You came to call sinners:
Christ, have mercy.
C: **Christ, have mercy.**

P: You plead for us at the right hand of the Father:
Lord, have mercy.
C: **Lord, have mercy.**

P: May almighty God have mercy on us,
forgive us our sins,
and bring us to everlasting life.
C: **Amen.**

(Turn to page 6)

THE GLORIA

On most Sundays and certain other days, the Gloria is said or sung:

P: Glory to God in the highest,

P & C: **and peace to his people on earth.**

Lord God, heavenly King,
almighty God and Father,
we worship you, we give you thanks,
we praise you for your glory.

Lord Jesus Christ, only Son of the Father,
Lord God, Lamb of God,
you take away the sin of the world:
have mercy on us;
you are seated at the right hand of the Father:
receive our prayer.

For you alone are the Holy One,
you alone are the Lord,
you alone are the Most High,
Jesus Christ,
with the Holy Spirit,
in the glory of God the Father. Amen.

COLLECT

P: Let us pray.
There is a short pause for silent prayer, after which the Priest says, or sings, the Collect, to which the Congregation answers:

C: **Amen.**

Liturgy of the Word

THE FIRST READING

All sit and listen to the First Reading, at the end of which the Reader says:

R: This is the Word of the Lord.
C: **Thanks be to God.**

RESPONSORIAL PSALM

The Reader announces the Response. The Congregation repeats it after the reader, and repeats it again after each verse of the Psalm.

THE SECOND READING

On Sundays and some other days there is a Second Reading, at the end of which the Reader says:

R: This is the Word of the Lord.
C: **Thanks be to God.**

ALLELUIA

The Alleluia or Acclamation is now sung: otherwise it may be said or omitted. The Congregation stands.

THE GOSPEL

Before reading the Gospel the Priest prays quietly:

P: Almighty God, cleanse my heart and my lips
that I may worthily proclaim your gospel.

Aloud, he says:
P: The Lord be with you.
C: **And also with you.**
P: A reading from the holy gospel according to N.
C: **Glory to you, Lord.**

At the end of the reading he says:
P: This is the gospel of the Lord.
C: **Praise to you, Lord Jesus Christ.**
Quietly, as he kisses the book:
P: May the words of the gospel wipe away our sins.

THE SERMON

A Homily is preached on Sundays, holydays and other suitable occasions.

THE CREED

On Sundays and certain other days, the Creed is said, or sung, as follows:

P: We believe in one God,
P & C: **the Father, the Almighty,
maker of heaven and earth,
of all that is, seen and unseen.**

**We believe in one Lord, Jesus Christ,
the only Son of God,
eternally begotten of the Father,
God from God, Light from Light,
true God from true God,
begotten, not made,
of one Being with the Father.
Through him all things were made.
For us men and for our salvation
he came down from heaven:
by the power of the Holy Spirit
he became incarnate from the Virgin Mary,
and was made man.
For our sake he was crucified under
Pontius Pilate;
he suffered death and was buried.
On the third day he rose again
in accordance with the Scriptures;
he ascended into heaven
and is seated at the right hand of the
Father.
He will come again in glory to judge the living
and the dead,
and his kingdom will have no end.**

**We believe in the Holy Spirit, the Lord, the giver
of life,
who proceeds from the Father and the Son.
With the Father and the Son he is worshipped
and glorified.
He has spoken through the Prophets.
We believe in one holy catholic and apostolic
Church.
We acknowledge one baptism for the
forgiveness of sins.
We look for the resurrection of the dead,
and the life of the world to come. Amen.**

THE BIDDING PRAYERS *are now said.*

Liturgy of the Eucharist

A HYMN may be sung during the Offertory, or the prayers offering the bread and wine may be said aloud.

As he offers the bread:

P: Blessed are you, Lord, God of all creation.
Through your goodness we have this bread to offer,
which earth has given and human hands have made.
It will become for us the bread of life.

C: **Blessed be God for ever.**

Quietly, as he pours the wine and water into the chalice:

P: By the mystery of this water and wine
may we come to share in the divinity of Christ,
who humbled himself to share in our humanity.

As he offers the wine:

P: Blessed are you, Lord, God of all creation.
Through your goodness we have this wine to offer,
fruit of the vine and work of human hands.
It will become our spiritual drink.

C: **Blessed be God for ever.**

Quietly, as he bows before the altar:

P: Lord God, we ask you to receive us
and be pleased with the sacrifice we offer you
with humble and contrite hearts.

Quietly, as he washes his hands:

P: Lord, wash away my iniquity;
cleanse me from my sin.

He then addresses the Congregation:

P: * Pray, brethren, that my sacrifice and yours
may be acceptable to God, the almighty Father.

*In Scotland and Ireland: Pray, brethren, that our sacrifice…

C: **May the Lord accept the sacrifice at your hands
for the praise and glory of his name,
for our good, and the good of all his Church.**

THE PRAYER OVER THE GIFTS

The Priest now says, or sings, the Prayer over the Gifts, to which the Congregation answers:

C: **Amen.**

The Eucharistic Prayer

P: The Lord be with you.
C: **And also with you.**

P: Lift up your hearts.
C: **We lift them up to the Lord.**

P: Let us give thanks to the Lord our God.
C: **It is right to give him thanks and praise.**

PREFACE AND SANCTUS

The Preface varies according to the occasion and at the choice of the Priest. Then all say or sing:

P & C: **Holy, holy, holy Lord, God of power and might,**
heaven and earth are full of your glory.
Hosanna in the highest.
Blessed is he who comes in the name of the Lord.
Hosanna in the highest.

Prayer III

Father, you are holy indeed,
and all creation rightly gives you praise.
All life, all holiness comes from you
through your Son, Jesus Christ our Lord,
by the working of the Holy Spirit.

From age to age you gather a people to yourself,
so that from east to west
a perfect offering may be made
to the glory of your name.

And so, Father, we bring you these gifts.
We ask you to make them holy by the power of your Spirit,
that they may become the body and blood
of your Son, our Lord Jesus Christ,
at whose command we celebrate this eucharist.

On the night he was betrayed,
he took bread and gave you thanks and praise.
He broke the bread, gave it to his disciples, and said:
Take this, all of you, and eat it:
this is my body which will be given up for you.

When supper was ended, he took the cup.
Again he gave you thanks and praise,
gave the cup to his disciples, and said:

Take this, all of you, and drink from it:
this is the cup of my blood,
the blood of the new and everlasting covenant.
It will be shed for you and for all
so that sins may be forgiven.
Do this in memory of me.

The priest invites the Congregation:

P: Let us proclaim the mystery of faith:

The Congregation takes up one of these Acclamations:

1 **Christ has died,**
Christ is risen,
Christ will come again.

2 **Dying you destroyed our death,**
rising you restored our life.
Lord Jesus, come in glory.

3 **When we eat this bread and drink this cup,**
we proclaim your death, Lord Jesus,
until you come in glory.

4 **Lord, by your cross and resurrection**
you have set us free.
You are the Saviour of the world.

5 In Ireland only
My Lord and my God.

Father, calling to mind the death your Son endured for our salvation,
his glorious resurrection and ascension into heaven,
and ready to greet him when he comes again,
we offer you in thanksgiving this holy and living sacrifice.

Look with favour on your Church's offering,
and see the Victim whose death has reconciled us to yourself.
Grant that we, who are nourished by his body and blood,
may be filled with his Holy Spirit,
and become one body, one spirit in Christ.

May he make us an everlasting gift to you
and enable us to share in the inheritance of your saints,
with Mary, the virgin Mother of God;
with the apostles, the martyrs,
(Saint N.) and all your saints,
on whose constant intercession we rely for help.

Lord, may this sacrifice,
which has made our peace with you,
advance the peace and salvation of all the world.
Strengthen in faith and love your pilgrim Church on earth;
your servant, Pope N., our bishop N.,
and all the bishops,
with the clergy and the entire people your Son has gained for you.
Father, hear the prayers of the family you have gathered here before you.
In mercy and love unite all your children wherever they may be.

(In Masses for the dead see facing page)

Welcome into your kingdom our departed brothers and sisters,
and all who have left this world in your friendship.
We hope to enjoy for ever the vision of your glory,
through Christ our Lord, from whom all good things come.

Through him,
with him,
in him,
in the unity of the Holy Spirit,
all glory and honour is yours,
almighty Father,
for ever and ever.

C: **Amen.**

(Turn to page 14)

In Masses for the cead the following may be said.

Remember N.
In baptism he (she) died with Christ:
may he (she) also share his resurrection,
when Christ will raise our mortal bodies
and make them like his own in glory.

Welcome into your kingdom our departed brothers and sisters,
and all who have left this world in your friendship.
There we hope to share in your glory
when every tear wil be wiped away.
On that day we shall see you, our God, as you are.
We shall become like you
and praise you for ever through Christ our Lord,
from whom all good things come.

Through him,
with him,
in him,
in the unity of the Holy Spirit,
all glory and honour is yours,
almighty Father,
for ever and ever.

C: **Amen.**

Communion Rite

THE LORD'S PRAYER

(Musical setting, page 32)

P: Let us pray with confidence to the Father
in the words our Saviour gave us:

P & C: **Our Father, who art in heaven,**
hallowed be thy name.
Thy kingdom come.
Thy will be done on earth, as it is in heaven.
Give us this day our daily bread,
and forgive us our trespasses,
as we forgive those who trespass against us,
and lead us not into temptation,
but deliver us from evil.

P: Deliver us, Lord, from every evil,
and grant us peace in our day.
In your mercy keep us free from sin
and protect us from all anxiety
as we wait in joyful hope
for the coming of our Saviour, Jesus Christ.

C: **For the kingdom, the power, and the glory are yours, now and for ever.**

THE RITE OF PEACE

P: Lord Jesus Christ, you said to your apostles:
I leave you peace, my peace I give you.
Look not on our sins, but on the faith of your Church,
and grant us the peace and unity of your kingdom
where you live for ever and ever.
C: **Amen.**

P: The peace of the Lord be with you always.
C: **And also with you.**

The Priest may now invite the people to greet one another:

P: Let us offer each other the sign of peace.

AGNUS DEI

The Agnus Dei is said or sung as the Priest takes the host, breaks it and places a small piece in the chalice.

C: **Lamb of God, you take away the sins of the world:
have mercy on us.
Lamb of God, you take away the sins of the world:
have mercy on us.
Lamb of God, you take away the sins of the world:
grant us peace.**

The Priest prays quietly:

P: May this mingling of the body and blood of our
Lord Jesus Christ
bring eternal life to us who receive it.

Then, either:

P: Lord Jesus Christ, Son of the living God,
by the will of the Father and the work of the
Holy Spirit
your death brought life to the world.
By your holy body and blood
free me from all my sins and from every evil.
Keep me faithful to your teaching,
and never let me be parted from you.

or

P: Lord Jesus Christ,
with faith in your love and mercy
I eat your body and drink your blood.
Let it not bring me condemnation,
but health in mind and body.

HOLY COMMUNION

The Priest raises the host slightly and addresses the Congregation:

P: This is the Lamb of God
who takes away the sins of the world.
Happy are those who are called to his supper.

P & C: **Lord, I am not worthy to receive you,
but only say the word and I shall be healed.**

At his own Communion the Priest prays quietly:

P: May the body of Christ bring me to everlasting life.
May the blood of Christ bring me to everlasting life.

A HYMN may be sung during Communion, or the Communion Antiphon said or sung. To each communicant the Priest says:

Priest: The body of Christ.
Communicant: **Amen.**

THANKSGIVING

After Communion a period of silence may be observed, or a hymn or a psalm may be sung.

As he purifies the chalice the Priest prays quietly:

P: Lord, may I receive these gifts in purity of heart.
May they bring me healing and strength, now and for ever.

POST-COMMUNION

P: Let us pray.

If there has been no silent prayer, the Priest pauses, then says, or sings, the Post-Communion, to which the Congregation answers:

C: **Amen.**

Concluding Rite

THE PARISH NOTICES *may now be announced.*

THE BLESSING

On certain occasions a more solemn form of blessing may be said or a special Prayer over the People may precede the blessing. The simple blessing is as follows:

P: The Lord be with you.
C: **And also with you.**

P: May almighty God bless you, the Father, and the Son, and the Holy Spirit.
C: **Amen.**

THE DISMISSAL

The Congregation is dismissed in one of the following forms:

P: Go in the peace of Christ.
or
P: The Mass is ended, go in peace.
or
P: Go in peace to love and serve the Lord.
C: **Thanks be to God.**

A HYMN *may be sung.*

The Eucharistic Prayers

Eucharistic Prayer I

P: The Lord be with you.
C: **And also with you.**

P: Lift up your hearts.
C: **We lift them up to the Lord.**

P: Let us give thanks to the Lord our God.
C: **It is right to give him thanks and praise.**

PREFACE AND SANCTUS

The Preface varies according to the occasion and at the choice of the priest. Then all say or sing:

P & C: **Holy, holy, holy Lord, God of power and might,
heaven and earth are full of your glory.
Hosanna in the highest.**

**Blessed is he who comes in the name of the Lord.
Hosanna in the highest.**

THE PRAYER

We come to you, Father,
with praise and thanksgiving,
through Jesus Christ your Son.
Through him we ask you to accept and bless
these gifts we offer you in sacrifice.
We offer them for your holy catholic Church,
watch over it, Lord, and guide it;
grant it peace and unity throughout the world.
We offer them for N. our Pope,
for N. our bishop,
and for all who hold and teach the catholic faith
that comes to us from the apostles.

Remember, Lord, your people,
especially those for whom we now pray, N. and N.

(Pray silently for the living)

Remember all of us gathered here before you.
You know how firmly we believe in you
and dedicate ourselves to you.
We offer you this sacrifice of praise
for ourselves and those who are dear to us.
We pray to you, our living and true God,
for our well-being and redemption.

Communicantes

(At Christmas, Epiphany, Easter, Ascension & Pentecost: see box opposite)

In union with the whole Church
we honour Mary,
the ever-virgin mother of Jesus Christ our Lord and God.

† We honour Joseph, her husband,
the apostles and martyrs
Peter and Paul, Andrew.

*[James, John, Thomas,
James, Philip,
Bartholomew, Matthew, Simon and Jude;
we honour Linus, Cletus, Clement, Sixtus,
Cornelius, Cyprian, Lawrence, Chrysogonus,
John and Paul, Cosmas and Damian]

and all the saints.
May their merits and prayers
gain us your constant help and protection.

[Through Christ our Lord. Amen.]

Hanc Igitur

(At Easter & Pentecost: see box opposite)

Father, accept this offering
from your whole family.
Grant us your peace in this life,
save us from final damnation,
and count us among those you have chosen.

[Through Christ our Lord. Amen.]

---

*Sections in square brackets may be omitted throughout.

SPECIAL COMMUNICANTES

Christmas and octave:
In union with the whole Church
we celebrate that day (night)
when Mary without loss of her virginity
gave this world its saviour.
We honour her,
the ever-virgin mother of Jesus Christ our Lord and God. †

Epiphany:
In union with the whole Church
we celebrate that day
when your only Son,
sharing your eternal glory,
showed himself in a human body.
We honour Mary,
the ever-virgin mother of Jesus Christ our Lord and God. †

Easter and octave:
In union with the whole Church
we celebrate that day (night)
when Jesus Christ, our Lord,
rose from the dead in his human body.
We honour Mary,
the ever-virgin mother of Jesus Christ our Lord and God. †

Ascension:
In union with the whole Church
we celebrate that day
when your only Son, our Lord,
took his place with you
and raised our frail human nature to glory.
We honour Mary,
the ever-virgin mother of Jesus Christ our Lord and God. †

Pentecost:
In union with the whole Church
we celebrate the day of Pentecost
when the Holy Spirit appeared to the apostles
in the form of countless tongues.
We honour Mary,
the ever-virgin mother of Jesus Christ our Lord and God. †

SPECIAL HANC IGITUR

Easter Octave, and Pentecost:
Father, accept this offering
from your whole family
and from those born into the new life
of water and the Holy Spirit
with all their sins forgiven.
Grant us your peace. . . . . . .

Bless and approve our offering;
make it acceptable to you,
an offering in spirit and in truth.
Let it become for us
the body and blood of Jesus Christ,
your only Son, our Lord.

The day before he suffered
he took bread in his sacred hands
and looking up to heaven,
to you, his almighty Father,
he gave you thanks and praise.

He broke the bread,
gave it to his disciples, and said:

Take this, all of you, and eat it:
this is my body which will be given up for you.

When supper was ended,
he took the cup.
Again he gave you thanks and praise,
gave the cup to his disciples, and said:

Take this, all of you, and drink from it:
this is the cup of my blood,
the blood of the new and everlasting covenant.
It will be shed for you and for all
so that sins may be forgiven.
Do this in memory of me.

The Priest invites the Congregation:

P: Let us proclaim the mystery of faith:

The Congregation takes up one of these Acclamations:

1 **Christ has died,**
Christ is risen,
Christ will come again.

2 **Dying you destroyed our death,**
rising you restored our life.
Lord Jesus, come in glory.

3 **When we eat this bread and drink this cup,**
we proclaim your death, Lord Jesus,
until you come in glory.

4 **Lord, by your cross and resurrection**
you have set us free.
You are the Saviour of the world.

5 In Ireland only
My Lord and my God.

Father, we celebrate the memory of Christ, your Son.
We, your people and your ministers,

recall his passion,
his resurrection from the dead,
and his ascension into glory;
and from the many gifts you have given us
we offer to you, God of glory and majesty,
this holy and perfect sacrifice:
the bread of life
and the cup of eternal salvation.

Look with favour on these offerings
and accept them as once you accepted
the gifts of your servant Abel,
the sacrifice of Abraham, our father in faith,
and the bread and wine offered by your priest
Melchisedech.

Almighty God,
we pray that your angel may take this sacrifice
to your altar in heaven.
Then, as we receive from this altar
the sacred body and blood of your Son,
let us be filled with every grace and blessing.
[Through Christ our Lord. Amen.]

Remember, Lord, those who have died
and have gone before us marked with the sign of faith,
especially those for whom we now pray, N. and N.
(Pray silently for the dead)

May these, and all who sleep in Christ,
find in your presence
light, happiness, and peace.
[Through Christ our Lord. Amen.]

For ourselves, too, we ask
some share in the fellowship of your apostles and
martyrs,
with John the Baptist, Stephen, Matthias, Barnabas,
[Ignatius, Alexander, Marcellinus, Peter,
Felicity, Perpetua, Agatha, Lucy,
Agnes, Cecilia, Anastasia]
and all the saints.

Though we are sinners,
we trust in your mercy and love.
Do not consider what we truly deserve,
but grant us your forgiveness.

Through Christ our Lord
you give us all these gifts.
You fill them with life and goodness,
you bless them and make them holy.

Through him,
with him,
in him,
in the unity of the Holy Spirit,
all glory and honour is yours,
almighty Father,
for ever and ever.

C: **Amen.**

(Turn to page 14)

Eucharistic Prayer II

P: The Lord be with you.
C: **And also with you.**

P: Lift up your hearts.
C: **We lift them up to the Lord.**

P: Let us give thanks to the Lord our God.
C: **It is right to give him thanks and praise.**

SPECIAL PREFACE

(Some other Preface may be used)

P: Father, it is our duty and our salvation,
always and everywhere
to give you thanks
through your beloved Son, Jesus Christ.

He is the Word through whom you made the universe,
the Saviour you sent to redeem us.
By the power of the Holy Spirit
he took flesh and was born of the Virgin Mary.

For our sake he opened his arms on the cross;
he put an end to death
and revealed the resurrection.
In this he fulfilled your will
and won for you a holy people.

And so we join the angels and the saints
in proclaiming your glory
as we sing (say) :

P & C: **Holy, holy, holy Lord, God of power and might,
heaven and earth are full of your glory.
Hosanna in the highest.**

**Blessed is he who comes in the name of the Lord.
Hosanna in the highest.**

THE PRAYER

Lord, you are holy indeed,
the fountain of all holiness.
Let your Spirit come upon these gifts to make them holy,

so that they may become for us
the body and blood of our Lord, Jesus Christ.

Before he was given up to death,
a death he freely accepted,
he took bread and gave you thanks.
He broke the bread,
gave it to his disciples, and said:
Take this, all of you, and eat it:
this is my body which will be given up for you.

When supper was ended, he took the cup.
Again he gave you thanks and praise,
gave the cup to his disciples, and said:

Take this, all of you, and drink from it:
this is the cup of my blood,
the blood of the new and everlasting covenant.
It will be shed for you and for all
so that sins may be forgiven.
Do this in memory of me.

The Priest invites the Congregation:

P: Let us proclaim the mystery of faith:

The Congregation takes up one of these Acclamations:

1 **Christ has died,**
Christ is risen,
Christ will come again.

2 **Dying you destroyed our death,**
rising you restored our life.
Lord Jesus, come in glory.

3 **When we eat this bread and drink this cup,**
we proclaim your death, Lord Jesus,
until you come in glory.

4 **Lord, by your cross and resurrection**
you have set us free.
You are the Saviour of the world.

In Ireland only

5 **My Lord and my God.**

In memory of his death and resurrection,
we offer you, Father, this life-giving bread,
this saving cup.
We thank you for counting us worthy
to stand in your presence and serve you.
May all of us who share in the body and blood of Christ
be brought together in unity by the Holy Spirit.

Lord, remember your Church throughout the world;
make us grow in love,
together with N. our Pope,
N. our bishop, and all the clergy.

> In Masses for the dead the following may be added:
> Remember N., whom you have called from this life.
> In baptism he (she) died with Christ:
> may he (she) also share his resurrection.

Remember our brothers and sisters
who have gone to their rest
in the hope of rising again;
bring them and all the departed
into the light of your presence.
Have mercy on us all;
make us worthy to share eternal life
with Mary, the virgin mother of God,
with the apostles, and with all the saints
who have done your will throughout the ages.
May we praise you in union with them,
and give you glory
through your Son, Jesus Christ.

Through him,
with him,
in him,
in the unity of the Holy Spirit,
all glory and honour is yours,
almighty Father,
for ever and ever.

C: **Amen.**

(Turn to page 14)

Eucharistic Prayer IV

P: The Lord be with you.

C: **And also with you.**

P: Lift up your hearts.

C: **We lift them up to the Lord.**

P: Let us give thanks to the Lord our God.

C: **It is right to give him thanks and praise.**

SPECIAL PREFACE

(No other Preface may be used)

P: Father in heaven, it is right that we should give you thanks and glory:
you alone are God, living and true.
Through all eternity you live in unapproachable light.
Source of life and goodness, you have created all things, to fill your creatures with every blessing
and lead all men to the joyful vision of your light.
Countless hosts of angels stand before you to do your will;
they look upon your splendour
and praise you, night and day.
United with them, and in the name of every creature under heaven,
we too praise your glory as we sing (say):

P & C: **Holy, holy, holy Lord, God of power and might,**
heaven and earth are full of your glory.
Hosanna in the highest.

Blessed is he who comes in the name of the Lord.
Hosanna in the highest.

THE PRAYER

Father, we acknowledge your greatness:
all your actions show your wisdom and love.
You formed man in your own likeness
and set him over the whole world
to serve you, his creator,
and to rule over all creatures.
Even when he disobeyed you and lost your friendship
you did not abandon him to the power of death,
but helped all men to seek and find you.
Again and again you offered a covenant to man,
and through the prophets taught him to hope for salvation.

Father, you so loved the world
that in the fullness of time you sent your only Son to be
our Saviour.

He was conceived through the power of the Holy Spirit,
and born of the Virgin Mary,
a man like us in all things but sin.
To the poor he proclaimed the good news of salvation,
to prisoners, freedom,
and to those in sorrow, joy.
In fulfilment of your will
he gave himself up to death;
but by rising from the dead,
he destroyed death and restored life.
And that we might live no longer for ourselves but for him,
he sent the Holy Spirit from you, Father,
as his first gift to those who believe,
to complete his work on earth
and bring us the fullness of grace.

Father, may this Holy Spirit sanctify these offerings.
Let them become the body and blood of Jesus Christ
our Lord
as we celebrate the great mystery
which he left us as an everlasting covenant.

He always loved those who were his own in the world.
When the time came for him to be glorified by you,
his heavenly Father,
he showed the depth of his love.

While they were at supper,
he took bread, said the blessing, broke the bread
and gave it to his disciples, saying:

Take this, all of you, and eat it:
this is my body which will be given up for you.

In the same way, he took the cup, filled with wine.
He gave you thanks, and giving the cup to his disciples, said:

Take this, all of you, and drink from it:
this is the cup of my blood,
the blood of the new and everlasting covenant.
It will be shed for you and for all
so that sins may be forgiven.
Do this in memory of me.

The Priest invites the Congregation:

P: Let us proclaim the mystery of faith:

The Congregation takes up one of these Acclamations:

1 **Christ has died,
Christ is risen,
Christ will come again.**

2 **Dying you destroyed our death,
rising you restored our life.
Lord Jesus, come in glory.**

3 **When we eat this bread and drink this cup,
we proclaim your death, Lord Jesus,
until you come in glory.**

4 **Lord, by your cross and resurrection
you have set us free.
You are the Saviour of the world.**

5 In Ireland only
My Lord and my God.

Father, we now celebrate this memorial of our redemption.
We recall Christ's death, his descent among the dead,
his resurrection, and his ascension to your right hand;

and, looking forward to his coming in glory,
    we offer you his body and blood,
the acceptable sacrifice
    which brings salvation to the whole world.
Lord, look upon this sacrifice which you have given to
    your Church;
and by your Holy Spirit, gather all who share this bread
    and wine (or: this one bread and one cup)
into the one body of Christ, a living sacrifice of praise.

Lord, remember those for whom we offer this sacrifice,
especially N. our Pope,
N. our bishop, and bishops and clergy everywhere.
Remember those who take part in this offering,
those here present and all your people,
and all who seek you with a sincere heart.
Remember those who have died in the peace of Christ
and all the dead whose faith is known to you alone.

Father, in your mercy grant also to us, your children,
to enter into our heavenly inheritance
in the company of the Virgin Mary, the Mother of God,
and your apostles and saints.
Then, in your kingdom, freed from the corruption of sin
    and death,
we shall sing your glory with every creature through
    Christ our Lord,
through whom you give us everything that is good.

Through him,
with him,
in him,
in the unity of the Holy Spirit,
all glory and honour is yours,
almighty Father,
for ever and ever.

C: **Amen.**

The Lord's Prayer